Ebay

by Neo Monefa

Table of Contents

1. Introduction

A shop that offers nearly you can imagine—from vintage records to the most modern gadgets, from small collectibles to big motors—one online marketplace has it all. Being the language of this generation and the backbone of online buying and selling, it is undeniable that eBay has paved the way for everyone to go the route of appreciating the world's largest collection of items for sale. eBay is more than a shop, but it has grown to be a meeting place, a place where all buyers, sellers, and entrepreneurs can reach people from all over the world for a common purpose: trading and selling.

While there have been various local stores and online shops sprouting like mushrooms, because they are literally everywhere, eBay has still been on the top list of people from all over the world when it comes to having the best shopping experience. Members of eBay enjoy the variety of items that are available here, and when eBay talks about variety, they mean serious and extensive diversity of items that are up for grabs. Getting the value for your money and getting the best buys will be an easy, enjoyable experience as you can see photos, compare prices, read item reviews and feedback, and get an overview of which product is better than the other. With eBay, you get more choices; you get more chances of coming back to this marketplace for your next good buy.

eBay is popular among collectors, as there is no other marketplace that brings together all the rare collectibles that are deemed to be treasures for some people. Name it— vintage cameras, Soviet army service medals, vintage arcade games, and old records— eBay is a haven. A selection of the most interesting collections and new items, you cannot logout from eBay without wanting to buy anything.

2. eBay: A Place for Entrepreneurs

If you think eBay is just for the collectors, shopaholics, or for people who simply need something, then you are missing out a lot. eBay is a place for entrepreneurs and sellers too. No need to pay for monthly store rentals or for warehouse fees, people from all over the world can buy the items you are selling with a single click. Sellers at eBay just need to pay a minimal amount to list the items that you wish to sell. Forget about hidden fees or expensive costs, as eBay just gets a small percentage of the worth of the items you have sold.

With eBay, the things you consider your trash can be someone else's treasure. If you have the spirit of an entrepreneur, selling on eBay can be a very big step towards realizing your strengths and your ability as an entrepreneur. eBay allows you to communicate and exchange deals with people from all corners of the world. Living up to its mission of "providing a global trading platform where practically anyone can trade practically anything," eBay has undeniably made itself the largest online place to buy and sell. With more than hundreds of communities and thousands of members from all over the world, eBay is a phenomenal success in this age and time when everyone demands value for his money and when more people have gone the entrepreneurial route.

3. How to Become Part of eBay?

Bid, buy, or sell. You can do anything you want on eBay with just few steps. You simply need to do few steps and you are on your way to being one of the most satisfied customer or successful entrepreneur!

There are two accounts that you can set-up. If you simply want to purchase items from eBay, you can follow these steps:

- **Step 1:** Simply enter your information. You just need to enter your name, email address, and you need to choose an eBay user ID and password.

- **Step 2:** Submit your information, which means you have accepted the User agreement and Privacy Policy. You can also get communications from eBay and you agree that you are least 18 years old. You can change your preferences in eBay notifications in My eBay page after you have set up your account.

- **Step 3:** Review your confirmation. You simply need to verify and review the information you have entered. Click on the "Yes, continue" button or you can click "No, please send to another email address link."

- **Step 4:** That's it! You can now start your eBay shopping! You may need to enter other required information as you start purchasing or selling items.

You can also choose to create a seller account if you want to start selling listing items on eBay. Simply follow these steps and you will be all set for your entrepreneurial high!

- **Step 1:** Set up your seller account by confirming the personal information that you have submitted to eBay. You need to verify your identity and choose an automatic payment method for the fees you need to pay as a seller and for reimbursements. You can read through the eBay Buyer Protection Policy to understand more about the claims. Having your PayPal verified will also be helpful as eBay will need to confirm your identity and credibility as a seller.

- **Step 2:** You can now create your listing! eBay will guide you to ensure that you can make a list of the items that you wish to sell. You can provide description of the items and eBay can help you categorize them properly. eBay also helps you to give the proper and reasonable pricing for your items.

- **Step 3:** Start selling now! You can already sell the items on your list! Make sure that you read the rules for sellers and familiarize yourself with the eBay policies and restrictions so you know what to do and what not to do when completing a deal.

Joining the thousands of members of eBay is one big step towards achieving success in your business, or in finding the store that can give you everything you need!

4. Setting up a Paypal Account

The variety of items being sold on eBay is touted to be the biggest among all the other online marketplaces that are accessible. You are literally few clicks away from buying the items that you want. Once you have chosen the item you want to buy, you need to read the description of the item thoroughly to make sure that this is the product you are looking for. You can also ask the seller some questions if you wish to know more.

You also need to get the assurance that the item you wish to buy is from a reputable seller. You can check feedback on the seller and see his rating and score, as well as other reviews and comments given by previous buyers. While eBay is an enjoyable place to shop and get unique items, you also need to remember that eBay is open to third party sellers and you want to deal only with sellers you can trust. Sellers put up the option for buyers to bid or buy the item right away. You can wait for the other bids or you can complete and finalize your transaction once you click the *Buy it Now* button.

Paying for the item you have purchased is not difficult. The seller gives you options on the available electronic payment methods. Most purchases and sellers do not allow bank wire transfers, money orders, or check transactions. eBay has policies on its accepted payments methods.

While there are restricted payment methods, eBay ensures that both sellers and buyers will not have a difficult time because these methods are also convenient and accessible. Here are the guidelines and allowed methods:

- PayPal

- ProPay

- Skrill

- Paymate

- Credit card or debit card processed through the seller's Internet merchant account

- Payment upon pickup

- Bill Me Later

Most clients prefer to use Paypal, which is a guaranteed sure and safe way to pay for the items you have purchased on eBay. With Paypal, you simply need a credit card or bank account and email address. Paypal can also be used by sellers when they pack slips and ship labels.

Paypal is owned by eBay but both websites can function independently. Using Paypal with your purchases on eBay makes your payment method easier.

Here are the steps on how to start up your Paypal account and use it for your purchases:

- **Step 1:** Go to the Paypal site and choose the type of account that you need. You can choose whether you need a personal, premier, or business account.

- **Step 2:** Provide your personal information such as your name, address, email address and register. You will need to use your email address to login to your account.

- **Step 3:** You also need to verify your identity by providing your bank account information. You can give your credit card number or your debit card details. The verification process will need you to deposit a small amount of money to prove that you have an existing account in the bank that you have used as reference.

- **Step 4:** You can also choose to link your bank accounts to Paypal so you can easily transfer the money whenever you get money using Paypal. You can also use Paypal for online transactions.

You can follow these steps if you want to separately create a Paypal account. You can also directly set up a Paypal account on your eBay account by following these steps:

- **Step 1:** Go to your eBay account and navigate to "My eBay" page so you can see your eBay account's summary.

- **Step 2:** Go to the "Account" tab so you can start setting up your Paypal account.

- **Step 3:** Click "Paypal Account" to begin the registration process. If you already have a current Paypal account, you can just choose to link it with your eBay account. You can also create a new account from this tab. You will be directed to the Paypal site, and after providing all the necessary information, you can click the "Return to eBay" button.

- **Step 4:** In order for you to complete the linking process, you simply have to click the "Link my Paypal Account."

Setting up a Paypal account is very simple. You can easily do the steps to make sure that you can send and receive the payment faster and close your transactions safely and conveniently.

Start your eBay experience now by creating your own Paypal account! eBay is really all about convenience, access, and shopping rolled into one online marketplace. With Paypal, your transactions will be literally completed with just a few clicks!

5. Navigating your My eBay Page

Being a member of eBay allows you to do a lot of things. You can buy the items you want, you can sell, and you can trade with other members. To help you keep track of all the activities and deals you make, you can use the My eBay page. You can use this page in sending and receiving emails, updating your account information, and in tracking all the buying and selling activity that you do.

Navigating your My eBay webpage will help you be on top of your transactions so you will always keep track of everything you need. In eBay, it is important that you update your information, especially if you are a seller, as this helps in establishing your reputation and credibility, which will be helpful with your future transactions.

Here is a list of the tasks you can do when using your My eBay page:

1. **Check your activity logs.** The *Buy* tab shows you the items you have placed bid on, the items you have made offers on, and even the items where you lost your bids. The *Lists* shows all the items you are waiting for, the bids that you are watching, your saved seller list, saved search list, your wish list, and other lists that you have customized. The *Purchase History* tab shows all the items that you have purchased in a period of three years. The *Sell* tab contains the items that you have listed for sale, and the items you are currently selling.

2. **View or update your information.** Simply click the *Account* tab. This contains the information on your billing

statements and other financial transactions. There are other links in the *Account* tab such as the following:

- **Personal Information.** You can easily update your user ID, contact details, email and mailing address, password, and preferred payment method. You can also edit your *About Me* details using this tab.

- **Address.** You can change your shipping address, payment, and registration details.

- **Summary.** This contains all the important information about your seller account, as well as your balance and preferred payment method.

- **Communication Preferences.** You can choose and edit the schedule of your notifications from eBay. You can also choose how other members can contact you.

- **Seller Dashboard.** You can check this link to see how you are faring as a seller.

- **Feedback.** Read and review comments and feedbacks that you have received from previous clients.
- **Site Preferences.** Use this tab so you can update your general preferences, or even your seller account preferences.

- **Seller account.** This tab is very helpful if you want to see all the relevant information for your seller fees. You can also check any balances or existing statements if you have subscribed to certain eBay applications.

- **Paypal Account.** You can check relevant information about your paypal account.

- **Subscriptions.** You can use subscriptions to help you with your selling strategies.

- **Marketing tools.** You can change choose which marketing tools do you need in your selling activities.

3. **Check and respond to messages.** The *Messages* tab contains the messages that were sent to you by eBay and by other members.

4. **Choose the applications that you want to use to enhance your selling strategies.**

You can also customize your My eBay page and display what tabs and sections do you want to see on your page. Simply follow these steps:

- Step 1: Go to My eBay page.

- Step 2: Navigate to the *Page options* link.

- Step 3: Choose the sections or links that you want to display on your age.

- Step 4: Click *Apply.*

You can also choose the pages that you want to see first. There are pages that may be more important to you than your default page. Follow these steps so you can change the order of the pages you see.

- Step 1: Go to My eBay webpage.

- Step 2: Click the *change* link and use the drop-down menu so you can choose which page you want to show first.

- Step 3: click *Apply.*

You can also change the order of the sections on each page by following these simple steps:

- Step 1: Choose the section that you want to move.

- Step 2: Choose the *Edit* link.

- Step 3: Move the sections wherever you want it to be.

Navigating and using your My eBay page will help you in a lot of ways. You need to know all the information, details, and activities that you have made. This page will also give you an overview of your transactions, financial activities, and other communication methods that you have created. This will also help you in finding out more effective selling strategies and your information will always be updated in case buyers check your profile or if they want to see the feedback that previous buyers leave.

6. Understanding the Types of Auctions

eBay is an online marketplace for everyone, as it welcomes third party sellers and it serves as a haven for collectors, and a shopping destination for other members. eBay is different as compared to other online shopping stores as it is open to trading and auctions. If you are a seller, you can open your list for bidding, while if you are a buyer, you can place your bids and make an offer to the seller.

Auction is a big thing in eBay as this serves as one the backbone of its structure. eBay has introduced various type of auctions that are specifically designed to cater to the needs and preferences of the members. Every auction can serve its own advantages to every seller, and choosing the type of auction that will work best for your listings is now made possible. Some sellers would not want their items to be sold at a very low price, while some sellers would opt to sell these items in bulk, even at lower price.

As a seller, you need to know your objectives and the reason why you are selling the items on your list. Some sellers just want to move out their stuff from their home or from their warehouse, while some sellers really put too much value on the items that they sell. If you know what you want and you know the real value of your items, it would be easy for you to choose which type of auction will help you deliver and generate the sales that you want.

Here are the types of auctions which you can choose from:

1. **Normal Auctions.** These are the common auctions that you know wherein the buyers place their bid, some people can

outbid the offers, and finally, the winner of the bid gets the item. The regular type of auction is still preferred by most number of sellers and buyers because of its simplicity.

2. **Reserve Auctions.** If you do not want your items to be sold for a price that is less than the value you have assigned for it, you can do the reserve auction. If a buyer bids but he does not bid a price that meets your "reserve price" then they will need to bid again if they really want to buy the item. In case no single buyer meets your "reserve price," the auction gets cancelled, and you can keep the item. This type of auction is usually used by sellers for their items that cost more expensive. This is a selling strategy as the seller is already aware that the item is quite pricey but he still wants to encourage members to bid at a lower initial price.

3. **Fixed Price Auctions.** This is also referred to as the "Buy it Now" where the buyer does not have to undergo the bidding process and he can simply purchase by paying the seller's asking price. It can also mean that the buyers can undergo the normal auction. Some sellers would not even want the buyers to bother go bidding for the items that they want. These sellers simply indicate the pricing of all the items they want to sell so the buyers can directly purchase.

eBay has also modified this type of auction by adding the feature "best offer" wherein the buyers can get in touch with the sellers in case they want to negotiate for a price. As a seller, the fixed price auction will require you to pay extra fees. You need to choose which items should you offer on fixed price auctions and which items can be offered using the normal auction. You should remember, as a seller, that the Buy it Now rate must be 10% higher than the initial bid price made.

4. **Multiple Item Auctions.** This is also known as the Dutch auction which is considered to be a rare type of auction. The seller can sell more than one piece of a certain item. This is a quite complicated type of bidding and most buyers are not into the multiple item auction. If the seller has a bigger quantity of the item he sells, he can opt for the multiple item fixed price auction where he can advise how many pieces does he have and give a fixed price rate per piece. The buyer can now buy how many pieces he wants by simply choosing the *Buy it Now* option.

eBay has truly paved ways for sellers to create their own strategies in selling their items and getting the worth of the products that they sell. These types of auctions are very important to give the buyers more variety in terms of purchasing experience and even in the course of bidding itself.

7. Listing and Pricing Strategies

A lot of sellers have identified eBay as an effective way to strengthen their business and make it an avenue to expand their enterprise. eBay has successfully brought people together in their pursuit to be the biggest online marketplace to offer a wide variety of items from all over the world. While there is a much bigger opportunity in eBay for your business, you should also remember that eBay is an auction site and you need to use certain selling strategies that will help you build your reputation in the site, to promote your list, and to make sure that you attract bidders and buyers.

eBay is not a traditional business form and it has its own business model. It is important that your strategies are aligned with eBay's structure, as your traditional marketing strategies will not be all applicable on eBay. eBay will need you to list the items that you sell and to determine the pricing of these items. Since this is an auction site, you need to give a price that will encourage buyers to place their bids, and not to turn them off or discourage them, just because you might have priced your list unreasonably.

Here are some effective pricing strategies that you can use:

- **Determine a good starting price.** This is a significant step if you want to encourage a lot of bidding. If you have a low starting price, buyers will be attracted to place their bids and a great number of bids is a positive sign. eBay members usually use this as measure of the offer's desirability. Having a low starting price also means you can save money on listing fees as these fees also go up when you increase your starting price.

- **Your starting price should be cost-based.** As a seller, you should know how to protect your funds. To make sure you will get the proper returns, you should use the cost of the item as your starting price. However, you should be careful in choosing which items where you are going to apply this starting price.

- **Determine a "buy it now" price.** Having a "buy it now" price will be helpful whenever there are impulsive buyers who would immediately buy the item that they have chosen without the need to go the process of bidding.

- **Determine your reserve price.** This is considered to be the most important price as this will give you the guarantee that you will get the amount of the item that you want the item to be sold. This gives you the chance to sell your item at its proper price. However you should also consider that there are buyers who do not like the idea of reserve price and they do not even try to bid once they see that there is a set reserve for a certain item. You might want to consider determining a starting price that will already make you satisfied as a seller.

In choosing the best pricing strategies, it is important that you know the real worth and value of your item and that you should know your budget and budget constraints. You should be familiar with the worth of unique items such as collectibles, or other high ticket items that are really rare to find. You should get the best professional valuation for these products so you can sell them at a value that is worth the item.

Here is a list of listing strategies that will help you sell your items faster and easier:

- Describe the items your list clearly and correctly. You should be clear about the features of the item, and you should also be honest with the condition of the item and if there are damages, in case you are selling an old item. You need to describe the following details to make sure that you inform your potential buyers the actual condition of your item:

> Double Check Condition (Is this a new item, used, or gently used?) You need to be specific with the physical state of the item. Double Check Material or fabric of the item Double Check Name of manufacturer, year of production
> Double Check Color and style. Providing detailed measurements will be helpful so your buyer will know if this is the item that he needs. Double Check Special features of the product Double Check Storage details

- Provide the details of the type of payment methods and the credit cards that you accept.

- Provide the details of your shipping charges.

- Display attractive photos of your items. Make sure that the items are desirable and the photo will attract buyers to check your listing.

- Present your item creatively. It is recommended that you use creative words and ways on how to encourage your buyers to join the bidding for the items you are selling.

eBay is a powerful selling avenue, but you also have to make sure that your selling strategies will be effective in this online platform. Being updated with the modern and most relevant selling and listing strategies will be really helpful in your business.

8. Posting your First eBay Auction

Being a member of eBay gives you opportunities to earn and to shop. It is a very simple, accessible and convenient process where you just have to create an account and you can already start listing and selling your items. The most important thing now is posting your first auction on eBay.

When you are new to eBay and you have already registered your seller's account, you should consider your strategies in ensuring that you attract more buyers or bidders. No matter how attractive your item is, you should also consider your pricing strategies as buyers and bidders on eBay are smart enough to know if you are selling items based on their actual retail value or you are over pricing the items.

Using your seller account, simply follow the steps on how to sell a specific item. Choosing the best category for your item will help you be noticed by buyers. eBay also helps you in identifying which category should you use. Crating a creative title and a comprehensive description will also be helpful in selling your products. This is important so you can ensure that buyers can easily search for your items.

Before doing your first auction, you need to determine your starting price. The best way to attract buyers and bidders is to have a reasonable starting price which is attainable and desirable. The key in doing auctions is that the items you sell will not really end up being sold at a very low price. You need to be smart in pricing your items as well as in determining the length of the auction. The longer the auction, the more people are encouraged to bid and you can see that the price of your item increases over time.

You've just made your first auction on eBay! No need to worry if your items do not get to be sold right away, as there are other opportunities for you to make the item part of the list again. It is important that you create an auction page that covers all the information that your buyers need to know about your item. You can also use images of the items so you can also attract more bidders. It is normal that bidders will have questions on the items you sell, you should take time answering these inquiries so buyers will further appreciate the item and you also build your credibility as a seller.

Your auction page should also include the policies on shipping, refund, and the methods of payment that you accept. You should also give your contact information in your auction page. This is necessary in building your credibility and your reputation as a seller in eBay. If you want to make eBay as a long term avenue for you to sell your products, then you should be mindful of the strategies that you use for your first auction.

eBay will guide the buyer in the process of how they should send you their payment. It is recommended that you should be able to receive the payment first before sending out the item. This is also one way of protecting your business from other members who might be just be messing up with your account.

Once you have started with your first auction in eBay, you will surely enjoy listing and selling more items and you will eventually discover and apply more selling strategies. Your first posting on eBay can lead to more auction, more items, more earnings, and more clients reached all across the world. Make sure that you get it right!

9. Your eBay Reputation

With millions of people from all over the world doing business via eBay, with thousands of money involved in everyday sale, and with hundreds of transactions made every hour, eBay is undeniably the undisputed largest auction site in the world. There is no other online marketplace that can bring together buyers and sellers from across the globe and give them the opportunity to experience shopping like never before and to earn money without being confined by traditional forms of entrepreneurship.

eBay is a breakthrough innovation that transcends the challenges of distance and instead, it proves just how distance can actually make things work better, as people with the same interests get bonded by certain listings that are attractive for them. With the multitude of the site's members and the variety of items that are listed here, there is no stopping eBay from being the biggest thing in online shopping.

If you are a seller, you may be overwhelmed with the enormity of eBay, and you cannot fathom how buyers can reach you and how your business can grow in such a very big marketplace. Just like in traditional business model, you need to have marketing strategies on how to stay on top of the competition or on how to capture your market. With eBay, you also need to align your strategies with the website's business model. Despite these differences in strategies, one strategy remains to be the true to all business models—create a good and positive reputation.

As more and more people opt for online shopping, more doors open for consumers to be more expressive of their online shopping experience. The word of mouth now become digital as it is very easy to leave a comment or a feedback on a seller's page whether the customer liked or disliked their sale. This just emphasizes that today, more than ever, you should be more conscious, careful, and competent with how you conduct your eBay business. A single mistake or an oversight or neglect on your part can cost the reputation you have built for months or even years.

Here are some of the most effective strategies on how to build and maintain a good reputation on eBay:

- **Maintain a good relationship with your customers.** No matter how big or small the sale did your customer have, you should make him feel that you are sincere about giving him the quality item that he needs. You should also let him know that you are looking forward to your next transaction. If you give him the satisfaction from the sale, there is a big likelihood that he will share his experience with his friends and even encourage them to buy from you.
Happy customers find it easier to talk about your business, thus, the digital word of mouth comes into place and it works its wonders for your business without you having to pay for advertisements. Guarantee your customers' satisfaction and be ensured that they will help you in your promotion, even without asking them to do it.
- **Gain positive feedback.** With the availability and room for feedback, eBay encourages customers to leave their feedback on the transaction that they did with you. Remember that the feedback is visible to everyone so everything you do for your customers will surely be reflected in your page. Gaining positive feedback can give you increased ratings and you should aim to get the "trusted seller" title so it will be easy to pull more customers in. This is how big the impact is when it comes to delivering customer satisfaction and exceeding expectations.

- **Be honest and be clear in your item listing.** Your honesty about the items that you sell will surely go a long way. You should describe the items on your list clearly, while stating all the details that the customer needs and deserves to know. If the item is slightly used, and is not new, you should also give this information. Your item description should not just be a marketing promotion of an item which you probably have lost interest in and you just decided to sell it. The item description will be used by the customer as basis for his sale.

- **Reply to eBay inquiries promptly.** Customers are more likely to trust a seller who replies promptly to their queries. You should how them that you are serious about doing business with them, thus you earn for yourself a positive reputation. Being knowledgeable about your items also give you the authority over other sellers, hence, customers would prefer to do business with you.

- **Stay true to your shipping delivery date commitment.** Shipping and arrival of items are the key factors of the successes of most sellers in eBay. Customers want to get the item they paid for in the earliest possible time so you do not want to disappoint them with late postings and shipping.

These ways can be your everyday routine because that is how simple it is to make sure that your customers are happy and satisfied. A good reputation will take you to new heights and maintaining this reputation will surely make your business strong and growing.

10. Building Feedback

Just like any customer, you surely want to purchase items only from trusted eBay sellers. No matter how attractive the product is, if the seller has not received any positive feedback or positive ratings, you will hesitate on placing your bid or hitting that *buy it now* feature. Buyers and bidders need an assurance, a guarantee that they are purchasing from the right sellers, and that their purchases are really worth their money.

eBay is a powerful business tool and you need strong, effective, and creative selling strategies to ensure that you meet your sales targets and deliver beyond revenue. One way of ensuring that you are on top of the competition is to gather positive feedback on the previous transactions you have done with other buyers or bidders. Feedback is the most important basis and measure of a seller's credibility. Any buyer who reads a list of positive feedback about you will not waste a second hesitating whether to buy from you or not. Positive customer feedback serves as your advertising strategy which comes in free, and this free advertising happens to be the most effective tool, among the others.

Gathering a bevy of positive feedback cannot happen overnight, as you need to establish yourself first as a credible supplier by providing your customers quality items that meet their standards, while keeping the honesty and integrity in your transactions. If you are a beginner in eBay, you should not be discouraged as no matter how long the time it seems for you to be able to gather positive feedback, you will get there. And when you are there, you will surely appreciate every moment you took time to reach out to a customer, every note you left, and every feedback that they gave.

Working on Getting Positive Feedback

There are a lot of ways you can do to get positive feedback from your customers. Here are some of the most effective ways:

- **Establish your credibility in eBay.** People want to transact business with someone who knows eBay, with someone who knows how eBay works, a person who is no new to the business model. You can show that you are familiar with the rules in eBay by being a buyer, too. You can shop for cheap yet useful home items and leave feedback. This shows that you know your market and you know their behavior, which gives you the edge over the other sellers.

- **Prepare everything you need before posting your auction.** You need to pin down the details—right from the shipping procedures, your shipping company and its policies, it delivery schedule, the product packaging, product condition, and all the other product details. You need to set a high standard for all the products that you ship so you will not cause any disappointment to your customers. Preparing before your auction does not put you behind competition, but it gives you more reasons to strengthen your business. Firming up details such as shipping procedures shows that you are serious about delivering satisfactory service to customers, which then will give you positive feedback later on.

- **Complete your sale competently.** Make sure that you transact with your customers with competence, while still anchored on the fact that you should give them the value and worth of their purchase. If a customer contacts you or asks you, you should be accommodating enough to address all his concerns and you can even suggest other items that may be on your list.

- **Do not be afraid to communicate.** While a customer may be happy and satisfied with his purchase from you, he might not be too keen in leaving feedback or in answering a survey. Reach out to your customers by asking them their feedback on the transaction or trading.

- **Practice honest, correct, and fair trading.** No matter how good your items can be, but if the way you deal with your trading partners and business impedes the possibility of a good transaction, then you will never get good feedback. By being honest and fair to your customers, you give them the service that they need and they will easily express and share their satisfaction to the other members of eBay.

- **Sell the best items.** Never ship out or sell items that are not in good condition, expired, or damaged. Only one damaged item delivered to customer will cause damage to your reputation as a seller. Despite the other positive feedback, and you have one strong negative feedback on your list, customers will more likely think that you do not sell quality items.

- **Be meticulous.** Focus on every small detail of your eBay business. Do not let minor mishaps or mistakes slip out of your control.

Word of mouth is deemed to be the most effective form of advertising. Just like in any traditional business form, word of mouth also works for the eBay model. In this model, excellent customer service comes as first priority. In a big online platform like eBay, gaining the trust of your customers is truly a privilege.

11. 10 Steps to Successful Selling in eBay

Selling in eBay is not synonymous with merely opening a shop that sells everything you want to sell. There is a whole new science behind every successful eBay business out there. While you might have business strategies that you deem effective for traditional business, you need to make sure that you create new business strategies with your online business. eBay, as a big online platform can be both your advantage and disadvantage as a business. You need to learn how to use this online platform to your advantage so you can transcend the challenges of distance and communication.

Being a seller in eBay gives you the opportunity to let the world know that you have the best quality, unique, or versatile items that they need. With eBay, there is no limitation with the items that you sell, as you can from vintage to modern, from the smallest item, to big-ticket products. You can ship all the way from north to Asia, and vice versa. eBay opens bigger doors for your entrepreneurship, it gives you more opportunities to grow your business.

On top of everything, it is important to understand the eBay business model. It is an auction site therefore you expect people to display interest and to bid for an item that they want. As there are also direct purchases, you can also leverage on your pricing strategies so you can gain the edge over other sellers.

To guide you to a successful selling business in eBay, here are the ten steps you need to follow:

Careful and Strategic Product Selection

Having a shop in eBay does not necessarily mean selling everything on bargain. You cannot just sell everything altogether—from home items, to children apparel, to fashion items, to vintage collections. The secret to successful item listing is for you to identify your niche in the market. You need to determine your specialty as a store. What are your key products that remain the focus of your business?

Do you specifically sell gadgets? Fragrances? Apparel? You should stick to your specialty and avoid mixing up all the items you want to sell just because you want to earn. When you have the focus on the hero items that you sell, you earn credibility for that certain niche in the market.

The next step is choosing the niche that will give you the most successful financial returns. You should choose a niche that is not yet saturated. While it may be challenging to put up against competition, you should bear in mind that eBay cannot display all the listings that fall under a highly saturated category. By choosing a niche, you can leverage on unique items that can be your specialty in your store.

Correct and Effective Category Selection

After you have identified your products, you need to choose the correct category where you are going to have your items listed. You should position your item creatively. You need to categorize your items to its rightful category, where other items of its kind can also be found. Do a research first by researching for items that are same with yours. Determine which categories the other buyers have listed the items in. Make sure these are all active categories, and you can do this by hitting up the keyword search button.

You should also check the page-view counters and the activity and bidding involved in certain items in your chosen categories. This will help you measure the success of other listings in that category. You can easily determine if you got the proper category by being listed with other similar items. You can also choose to be listed in two categories.

Selection of Auction Title

Now that you have the products, niche, and category for your item listing, you also need to ensure that your listings get the visibility that you need. The title of the auction should be creative yet it should also focus on the keywords and all these should all be covered. Your keywords should all be significant to the category as well.

Creative and comprehensive auction description

A customer will always rely on the information that you will give him. Whenever you describe your auction, you should spark the interest of the customers and use a creative way of making your listings and items attractive. By being more specific with the listings, you also make searching for customers easier and faster.

Using attractive product pictures

Using eBay as an avenue for your business can somehow limit the customers' access to the actual products. There can be less appreciation because customers cannot actually see or hold the items. Uploading accurate, attractive, and nice pictures of the items that you are opening for auction will be a great help in encouraging customers to check out your products and place their bids. Using photos also gives you the credibility as a seller and helps you build your reputation. If you mean business, you need to show it to your customers as this will surely give them the confidence to start doing business with you.

Promote your business in all possible ways

eBay is an enormously big marketplace and for you to succeed, you need to promote your own business in all the opportunities possible. You may start by customizing your eBay ID to the actual name of your business site, if you have any. You can also publish your auction link on your own website. You can also post your contact details in your auction listings. Direct your customer to your other listings, make use of the "View seller's other items" feature.

You can enhance your list by putting various items in separate relevant categories and use cross promotion. This caters to a wider selection of potential buyers and let them know that you also have other items to sell. You do not need to promote a long list of items; listing only the most in demand products will surely boost your promotion. You can do your own promotion with these simple and cheap methods.

Shipping, handling, and insurance

Your buyers deserve to know your shipping and handling fees. You need to state your flat rate shipping costs or if you will use calculated shipping costs, which is based on size and weight of the item that you will ship. If the buyer wants to insure the item, you also need to state the insurance cost. Providing your buyers with other shipping options will also make them feel that you are prioritizing their needs. When customers ask you about your shipping and handling procedures, you should be open about it and answer them. It is also important that you do not charge your customers excessive shipping costs as this will surely taint your relationship with your customer and cause damage to your reputation.

Getting Paid using the best way

There are many ways on how to get paid on eBay and you need to give your customers at least one payment method. You can use electronic method or an internet merchant credit card. You can use PayPal, ProPay, Skrill, Paymate, Merchant credit card, or payment upon pick-up. These methods are safe and are traceable. Personal check, bank-to-bank transfers, and money order are not allowed on eBay. This gives you the protection from possible fraud.

Organizing your business

You need to keep records of all your auctions and all your eBay sales. You should not totally rely on eBay as eBay only stores your records for a limited amount of time. Organizing everything you need for your eBay business will help you in the long run, especially if you want to relist your items or put them up for auction again. You need to keep the following information: item number, bidder email and ID, the item sold, total fees paid on the item, the payment method used, and the feedback you received.

Research and pricing strategies

The success of your eBay business lies on your pricing strategies as well. You cannot entice and encourage your buyers and bidders if you list items that are too expensive, or if your starting price is so high. You need to thoroughly research on the appropriate pricing rates on the items you sell, especially if you are selling vintage or collectible items. This will help you keep your competency and your edge over other sellers.

These are the top ten ways on how to make sure that you are on top of the competitive group of sellers on eBay. Having a successful business on eBay entails a lot of research and strategic planning. You should leverage on eBay's network that reaches customers from across the globe. You can just imagine how thousands of buyers and bidders can be willing to place their orders and purchase your items, so you better make sure that all your strategies and plans are in place. Building your reputation in eBay is the first step towards creating a strong market and a group of loyal customers.

12. How to Think like an eBay Powerseller?

eBay is proven to be a good business model, as a growing number of entrepreneurs have established and expanded their businesses in eBay. eBay acknowledges competent and skillful sellers by naming them the "eBay Powerseller". eBay awards top rated sellers who are consistent with the quality of the items that they sell, with the positive feedback that they have been receiving from their customers, and with the standard of excellence that they maintain when doing their business.

eBay Powersellers are given special benefits and programs, however it takes a lot of effort and excellence to be awarded with such rating. Some of the benefits include discounts on final value fees, boost in Best Match search results, Top Rated seller badge on your item listings, UPS rate discounts. PowerUp email newsletters, and consultations on how you can maintain your Top Rated seller status. Maintaining your position and credibility as an eBay Powerseller is another story, and a much bigger responsibility.

How to qualify as an eBay Powerseller?

eBay will determine if you are considered to be a Powerseller or not. They have really strict qualifications and you need to meet all these requirements for you to be privileged to be awarded with this title. Here are the requirements you need to meet:

- You must gain a feedback rating of at least 100. Minimum feedback rating should be at 98%.

- You should sell $1000 worth of items minimum, for three months consecutively.

- Qualify for bronze level with a total worth of $1000, $3,000 for silver, $10,000 for gold, $25,000 for platinum, and $125,000 for titanium.

- Maintain your Powerseller status means you have to keep your monthly sales at these levels, and your feedback rating of at least 98%.

Being an eBay Powerseller cannot happen overnight. Once you attain that status, you need to work hard to maintain it. Not all entrepreneurs have the mindset o a Powerseller, because there are businesses in eBay that just operate at a regular pace, without going the extra mile or effort to improve its customer service. If you want to be a certified Powerseller, you need to start thinking like one.

Here are some ways on how to plan and act like a Powerseller:

- **Treat your eBay business as a serious business.** Being on eBay does not mean you are limiting yourself to an online platform. eBay is practically the biggest online marketplace of today so there is every reason to make sure you are doing well in your business. The whole world can see how you do strategize, how you execute your plans, and how you gain the credibility as a Powerseller.
  Your eBay business is not just a random selling of all the items you want to sell, but it should be a strategic way of listing, pricing, and encouraging buyers and bidders to take time to look at your auction page, and to actually put their confidence on the products that you sell.

- **Powersellers think long term goals.** They are not just after selling all the items possible, but they identify the appropriate and most effective listing that will bring success to their business. They lean towards selling the same items over time, and this gives them the credibility and stability. Just like in traditional businesses and the ordinary marketplace, there can be challenges in pricing, in market demand, or in preference, but an eBay powerseller knows just how to address these issues without compromising his business. Stability—that is the key secret of every eBay Powerseller. Without stability, he cannot maintain his status and his business will succumb over competition.

- **Choose the risks that you are going to take.** Some businesses are in hurry to grow, while a Powerseller does everything slowly but surely. You need to know which risks to take and the returns and outcome should be long-term and not just for instant spike in sales. You need to manage your business in such a way that your reputation, credibility, sales, and customer service are not compromised.

- **A Powerseller takes advantage of every opportunity for him to promote his business.** He thinks of strategies such as cross promotion, or linking his auction site to his website, or placing his contact numbers all over his auction page. He plans of using other avenues to let everyone know about his business. this means going the extra mile to call on potential bidders and buyers instead of waiting for them to stumble upon your site.

- **A Powerseller thinks beyond what is readily available.** He reaches out to his customers and makes them feel that they are important to the business. He seeks for their feedback and takes them as significant in improving his business and in maintaining his credibility.

Being an eBay Powerseller is not just a privilege, but an assertion of your responsibility to keep track of your business, of your performance, and of your products. It goes beyond giving buyers exciting offers or selling good items, but actually being the face of a strong business.

13. Opening an eBay Store

Selling on eBay allows you to tap a bigger potential market as you can reach customers from all over the world. It is not an easy money business because you have to come up with strategies that work for the site. Since this is not an ordinary business model, you have to realign your plans and make them work for eBay.

One of the key strategies when you have a listing on eBay is to open your own eBay store. If you are selling high volume items, in big quantities of a specific item, then opening your eBay store is one of the best strategies you can do. Having an eBay store allows you to list and categorize your products into its respective categories, so your customer can easily locate you and find the items that they want to buy. With your eBay store, you can also blatantly do your promotions, keep your relations with your customers by sending them newsletters, and you can also create more marketing strategies in here.

If you are consistently selling items on big quantities, you can save on money by having your own eBay store as you do not need to pay eBay whenever you need to re-list unsold items in the future.

What are the benefits of having an eBay store?

Having an eBay store is not just limited to PowerSellers, as even starters can open an eBay store for their business. Here are the advantages of having an eBay store:

- **Earn more profit.** Statistics show that sellers with eBay store experience an average increase of 25% in total sales within three months upon opening your store. The fees you pay for a store will help you save on auction fees when you do your regular auction business on eBay. Another good thing about having your eBay store is that you can do your own promotion and offers that you will not get to do when you are on regular eBay site. You can also offer subscriptions to your customers.

- **Establish reputation and credibility.** An eBay store will give you and your business the impression that you are a credible entrepreneur. The layout of your store should exude professionalism and credibility that will surely attract customers and encourage them to patronize your business. eBay offers templates for business cards and for other business materials that you can use.
eBay store owners have the access to the Business resource center.

- **Gain regular customers.** When you have an eBay store, it will be easier for customers to come back to you if ever they need more items. When they experienced a good customer service from you, it is more likely that they will be regular customers.

- **You can have your own link.** Having your own eBay store is like having your own website which you can promote all over. This will also be searchable in search engines, without having to redirect them to eBay's auction site.

- You can manage your own eBay store. You can manage the items and create categories. These categories will help your customers find the information and items that they need. You can also personalize the look of your store, and align it with the branding of your store.

- **You have your own search engine.** One powerful tool that you can have on your own store, to find your own items for sale is your very own search engine.

- **Get free monthly reports.** eBay provides all store owners reports on their monthly gross sales, number of buyers for the month, and their conversion rates. You can also get information against your competitors as eBay can also provide you with a general marketplace date. This will keep you ahead of everyone else because you can already plan what to do or you can already come up with strategies that will keep you on top of the competition.

Now that you have determined if you really need an eBay store and if you are ready to manage it, the next thing to do is to create your eBay store. You can follow these steps:

1. **Open your eBay store by having your own seller account.** There may be limitations for eBay sellers in terms of monitoring selling practices so you need to check if your account has limits. You also need a verified PayPal account.

2. **Subscribe to an eBay store.** You can choose the subscription level that you think your business needs. Choose the name of your store. Your store name is important as this will be your URL or your web address.

3. **Set up and customize your eBay store.** A professional looking store will surely attract more customers and will exude the credibility that you want them to feel. You need to make your store appealing and exciting. This will surely contribute to your sales. A polished look will allow your buyers to easily search for the items that they need. They will enjoy shopping and will be encouraged to come back to your shop.

4. **Start listing your items.** Since you have your own store, you can easily manage your own categories and listings. You can

use various listing tools such as the Turbo Lister or the Selling Manager Pro.

5. **Manage your eBay store.** You can now be in charge of your own store and manage your own promotions and listings.

6. **Promote your eBay store.** Create marketing and advertising call-outs that will entice customers to visit and stay on your page. You can determine or announce your own sale and be more creative with your offers.

Another important thing about having your eBay store is optimizing it so it will be easily searchable by customers. Here are some ways on how to optimize your eBay store:

- Choose a store name that will describe the items that you are selling. If you are selling gadgets and computers, it will be best to put these keywords on your store name. This will also make your store searchable by search engines so more customers can check out your site.

- Make sure that your store description provides the accurate idea of what are the products that you sell. It should contain keywords that are highly searchable by people. The store description should be enticing enough to encourage customers to check out your page and to take time visiting your other pages. Your store name and store description are like your door openers in attracting more customers to view your listings.

- Create custom pages. These pages will help advertise your promotions, your key offers, your hero products, and it can even give the customers a view of your business history. These pages can help in optimizing your website and in making sure that you will be present in top search results.

- Personalize and customize your categories. Now that you have the chance to create your own categories instead of just finding the best ones for you back at the eBay auction site, you should create categories that are popular keywords. They should be simple, direct, and clear.

- Assign popular search engine keywords. It will be best to create search engine keywords that your potential customers will search for.

As a good entrepreneur, you also have to know how to promote your eBay store using cheap but effective methods. Yes, there is an impressive bevy of advantages you can get from having your own eBay store but it does not stop there. You need to work on promoting it and letting everyone know that you have an eBay store and they should click the link, visit it, start their purchase, and come back for more purchases. Here are some ways on how to promote your store:

- Promote your store's URL upon the premise that your URL is a decent, concise and clear short description of the items that you sell. You can post the link of your store on your About me page. You can also do cross promotion if you have other websites.

- You can still have your regular auctions. This will give your site more mileage in terms of cross promotion. When bidders visit your store for an auction, you can also let them see and encourage them to check out your other items.

- Personalize your email signature and add your store's link so they can just easily click on it. This is literally taking every opportunity available in the market and in online platforms and making it sales generating.

With all these efforts in customizing, managing, and promoting your eBay store, how will you know if you are generating a fair amount of income and if you are effective in attracting customers and potential bidders to your store? eBay can provide you with a traffic report that shows the quantity of visitors that go to your store, what are the most viewed pages, the visitors' activities, and even the most popular search keywords that customers use.

Checking your traffic report will guide you on how to redesign your pages, in determining your search engine keywords, and in improving the layout of your store. eBay provides you with tools that will be helpful in making sure that your store will be frequented by your potential customers. Some of these tools and reports are free, all you have to do is to use them and to revisit your store once in a while and redesign or revise if needed.

Having an eBay store allows you to do a lot of things—from the simple customization to creating your own offers. By being a smart entrepreneur, you know how to maximize this store and promote it to everyone. You can get the mileage and the sales returns that you expect if you know how to properly strategize your plans and your actions.

14. THANK YOU FOR READING!

Thank You so much for reading this book. If this title gave you a ton of value, It would be amazing for you to leave a REVIEW !

THANK YOU FOR DOWNLOADING! IF YOU ENJOYED THIS BOOK AND WOULD LIKE TO READ MORE TITLES FROM MY COLLECTION CLICK THIS LINK